D0235734

GROWING UP IN WORLD WAR TWO
GETTING ABOUT

Catherine Burch

FRANKLIN WATTS
LONDON•SYDNEY

First published in 2005
by Franklin Watts
96 Leonard Street, London
EC2A 4XD

Franklin Watts Australia
Level 17/207 Kent Street
Sydney, NSW 2000

© 2005 Franklin Watts

Produced for Franklin Watts by
White-Thomson Publishing Ltd,
Bridgewater Business Centre, 210 High Street,
Lewes, East Sussex BN7 2NH

Consultant: Andrew Spooner, military historian
Design: Bernard Higton Design
Picture Acknowledgements: All photographs courtesy
of Getty Images – Hulton Archive.

A CIP catalogue record for this book is available from
the British Library.

ISBN 0 7496 6196 8

Printed in China

CONTENTS

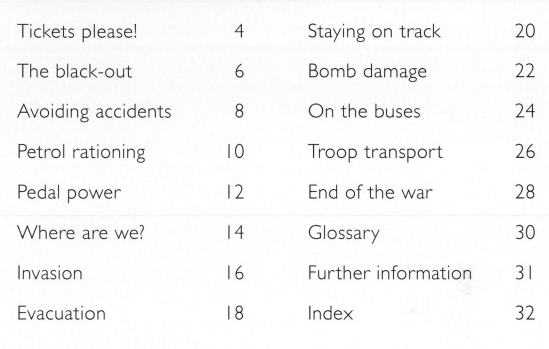

Words in the glossary are in **bold** the first time they appear.

TICKETS PLEASE!

Before World War Two (1939-45), getting about wasn't as easy as it is today. For example, not many people in the 1930s owned a car; they were an expensive luxury. There was not much traffic and roads were narrow.

People used buses and trains a lot more than we do now. Most people lived near their jobs, so they didn't travel about as much. They walked to work, or they caught a bus. Children walked or cycled to school, or also went by bus.

All steamed up, 1936
Passengers wait on a railway station platform before the war. The trains ran on steam – diesel trains were not introduced until 1948.

Busy buses, 1936
Londoners queue to board a bus. Some towns had trams or trolleybuses (buses powered by electricity from overhead wires) as well as ordinary, diesel-powered buses.

Picnic party, 1935
A family picnic in the countryside. In the 1930s, owning a car was a luxury that only wealthy people could afford.

THE BLACK-OUT

World War Two began when Nazi Germany invaded Poland. Britain declared war on Germany on 3 September 1939. The British government expected that there would be heavy bombing by German aeroplanes.

Britain therefore had a **black-out**. This meant that no lights could show from houses or on streets at night. People in houses and shops covered their windows with black paper or thick curtains so that enemy bombers could not see towns from the air. Streetlamps were turned off and the use of car headlights banned.

Lights out, 1939
A couple buy black-out cloth to cover their windows. **Air-raid wardens** made sure every building was properly blacked out.

Watch your step, 1939
In the black-out it was hard to see a car or bicycle coming towards you. Here, a policeman with a lamp helps people to cross the road safely.

I REMEMBER ••
'I remember... the scary journey to and from choir practice, as an eight-year-old in the black-out, in winter months. There were monsters behind every rhododendron bush on the way.'
•••••••••••••••••••• (John Soden, from The World War Two Memories Project)

AVOIDING ACCIDENTS

The black-out caused thousands of accidents, because people couldn't see where they were going in the dark.

They walked into rivers, fell down steps and toppled from railway platforms. The number of people killed on the roads doubled in the first month of the war. The government realised that banning car headlights was too dangerous. So drivers were allowed to use their headlights, but had to cover them with a mask so they gave off less light. Many people stayed at home after dark to be safe.

I REMEMBER ....
'I was never allowed to go to Brownies because it was held at the other end of town and my mother wouldn't let me walk there in the black-out.'

•••••••• (Joyce, aged 9, Biggleswade)

Warning signs, 1941
These boys have pinned white paper to their backs to make them easier to see on their walk home. It was dangerous for anyone to go out at night during the black-out.

Lamppost lines, 1939
Workers painted white lines on kerbs, trees and lampposts to make them easier to see.

PETROL RATIONING

During the war, German U-boats sank ships bringing supplies to Britain. This meant there were shortages of food, petrol and other goods that had to be imported from abroad.

The British government began to **ration** petrol. A small amount of petrol was allowed for private cars at first. The rest was given to those who needed it the most – the **armed forces**, farmers and lorry drivers. Later in the war, no petrol was allowed for private cars.

Midget miracle, 1939
One answer to petrol rationing was the midget car. This tiny car used very little petrol.

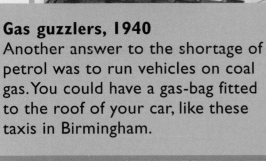

Gas guzzlers, 1940
Another answer to the shortage of petrol was to run vehicles on coal gas. You could have a gas-bag fitted to the roof of your car, like these taxis in Birmingham.

I REMEMBER ....

'Our local cinema was run by Mr Vincent Lockey, and owing to the petrol shortage he used an electric battery-driven van. It did about ten miles an hour on the level road and made a whining noise that was rather weird in the black-out.'

(Boy, aged 9, Humberside)

PEDAL POWER

One of the best ways to get about without using petrol was by bicycle. Many people cycled to work or school.

Cycling at night was very dangerous and frightening. It was hard to see the road, and car drivers could not see cyclists easily. There were lots of accidents. Not everyone had a bicycle, and it was difficult to buy one. Britain's factories needed to make guns, tanks and planes, rather than bikes.

Cycle city, 1939
This photograph shows people cycling to work in Portsmouth.

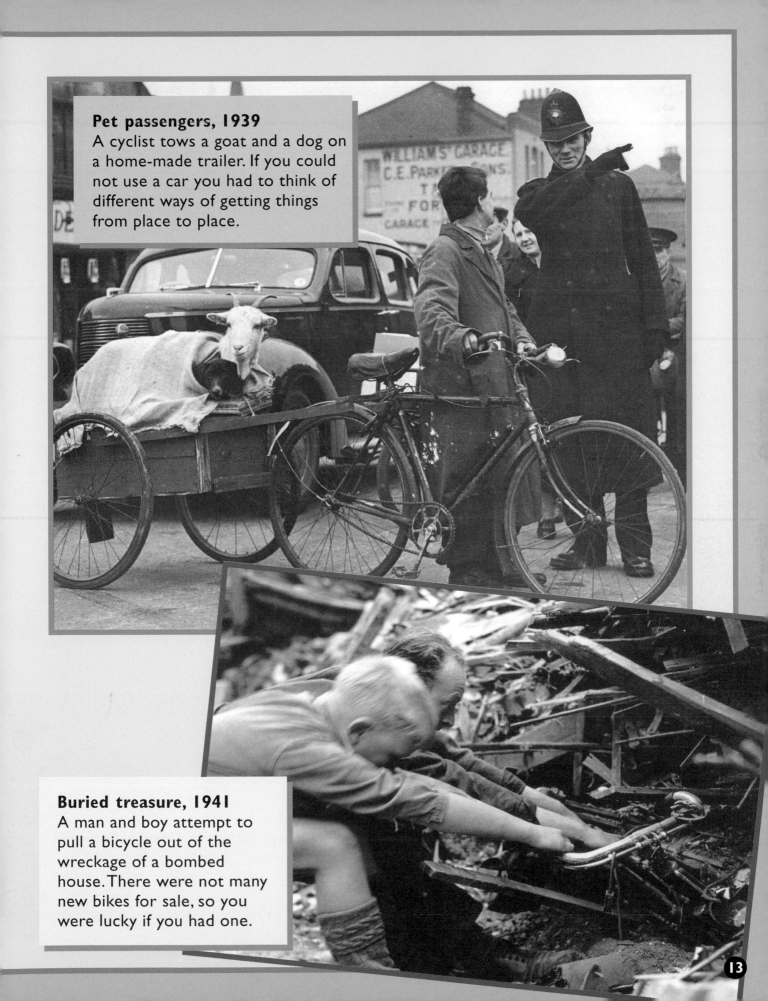

Pet passengers, 1939
A cyclist tows a goat and a dog on a home-made trailer. If you could not use a car you had to think of different ways of getting things from place to place.

Buried treasure, 1941
A man and boy attempt to pull a bicycle out of the wreckage of a bombed house. There were not many new bikes for sale, so you were lucky if you had one.

WHERE ARE WE?

Everyone was afraid that Germany would invade Britain. Signposts were taken down to make it difficult for invaders to find their way around.

Railway stations were not allowed to display the names of towns, so there were no signs on platforms to tell passengers which station they were at. Without signposts, everyone found it difficult to know where they were going.

Sign of the times, 1940
Workers remove a signpost in order to confuse the enemy. The British army soon had to ask for some signs to be put back to help them find their way!

Last-ditch defence, 1940
Barbed wire and soldiers guarded the coast to protect Britain from invasion. In many seaside areas it became impossible for people to visit the beach.

INVASION

Throughout the war, there were many rumours of German soldiers secretly arriving by parachute. Roadblocks were set up in country lanes, both to stop any invasion attempt and to check people's identities.

Some roadblocks were just broken-down cars or piles of old tyres. Others were huge blocks of concrete ready to drag on to the road. When the war started, everyone was given an identity card, which showed their name, age and address. A person's identity card helped to prove that he or she was not a German invader!

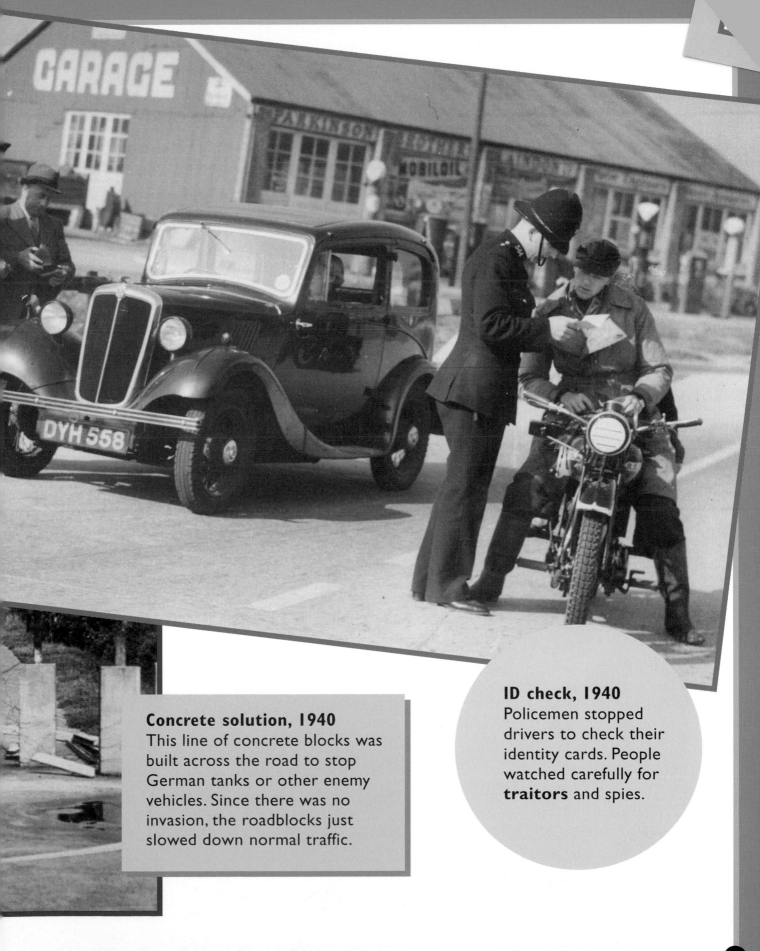

ID check, 1940
Policemen stopped drivers to check their identity cards. People watched carefully for **traitors** and spies.

Concrete solution, 1940
This line of concrete blocks was built across the road to stop German tanks or other enemy vehicles. Since there was no invasion, the roadblocks just slowed down normal traffic.

EVACUATION

During the war, the German air force bombed British towns and cities. As a result, the government evacuated millions of children to safer parts of the country.

No one was forced to evacuate, but parents were told it was for the best. Whole schools were often evacuated together. Most **evacuees** travelled by train. Some of the journeys were very long, and the children did not know where they were going. It was a frightening time.

Leaving home, 1939
Young children prepare to board a train to be evacuated to the safety of the country.

'We marched from our schools to the station, complete with gas mask and lapel labels ... When the train departed, the wailing and tears echoed up and down the train.'

.... (Boy, aged 6, North Shields)

All aboard, 1939
Children get on a bus to go to a railway station. The children all carry a **gas mask** in a box around their neck. People in cities were very afraid of poison gas attacks at the beginning of the war, but luckily they never happened.

Off to Australia, 1940
Families board a ship bound for Australia. Some people thought it would be safest to go abroad during the war.

STAYING ON TRACK

Many people travelled on long journeys by train. Trains were full of soldiers returning home on leave, or evacuees travelling to safety in the country.

Families going on holiday also went by rail. The number of people travelling meant that trains were often late and overcrowded. Old trains and carriages could not be replaced, because any spare metal was needed for making guns and planes to fight the war.

Holiday horrors, 1943
A crowd of people going on holiday waits for a train. Trains had to be blacked-out at night, and the lights were dimmed inside the carriages.

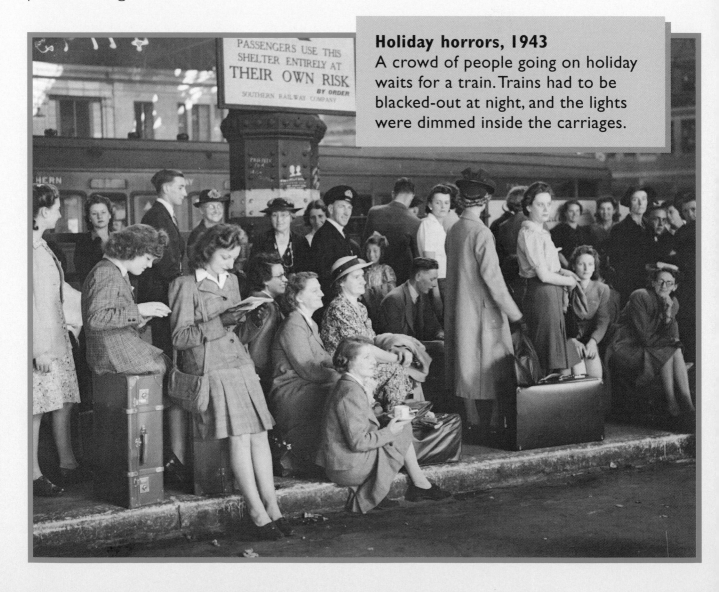

Home time, 1943
Soldiers at a London station head home **on leave**. Trains were always full of soldiers and other people in uniform.

BOMB DAMAGE

The damage caused by bombing made getting about much more difficult, whether by train, bus or car. The enemy dropped bombs on many roads, railway lines and stations.

When a bomb landed on a road it damaged the road surface and also the cables and pipes that ran underneath. Burst drains or water mains and damaged electricity cables had to be repaired before the road could be rebuilt.

Blitzed bridge, 1941
This city railway bridge was wrecked after a bomb hit it.

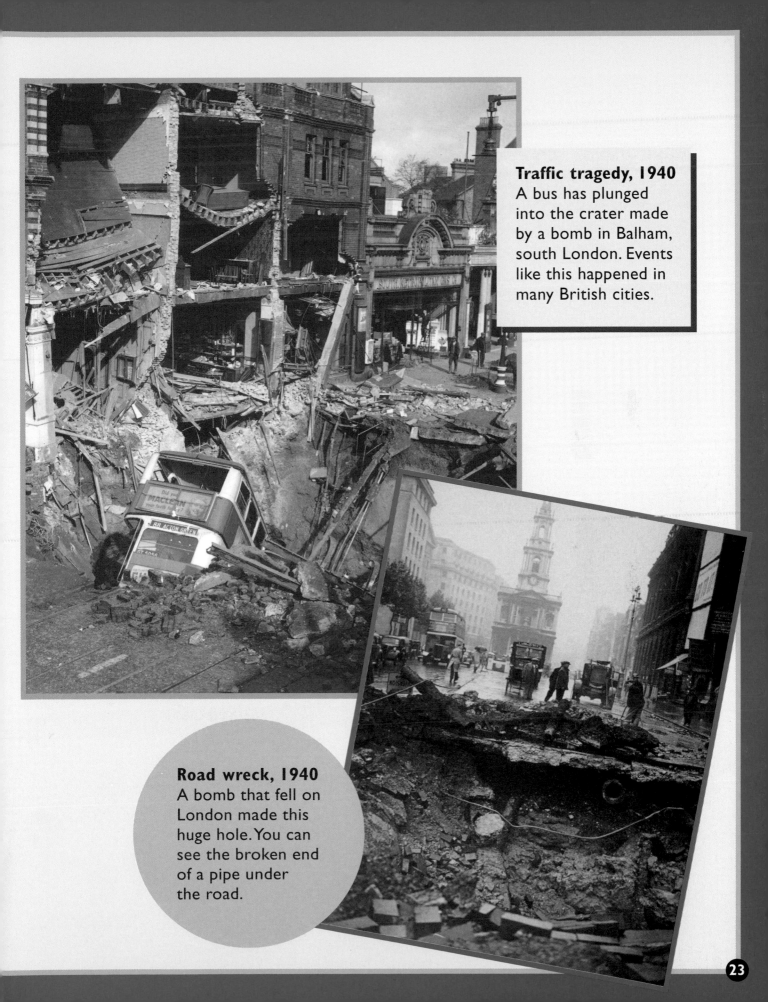

Traffic tragedy, 1940
A bus has plunged into the crater made by a bomb in Balham, south London. Events like this happened in many British cities.

Road wreck, 1940
A bomb that fell on London made this huge hole. You can see the broken end of a pipe under the road.

ON THE BUSES

Many people got about by bus during the war. There were not enough buses or staff, so vehicles were often crowded.

In London so many buses were damaged by the **Blitz** that vehicles had to be borrowed from other towns. There were very long queues at some bus stops, but people remained cheerful and strangers talked to each other more than usual. It was quite dark on a bus in the black-out. You could hardly see your money to pay the conductor!

Fares, please! 1941
Many male bus drivers and conductors joined the armed forces. Women took over their jobs.

Just in case, 1941
People at a bus stop wear gas masks for a **gas practice**. At the beginning of the war everyone had to carry a gas mask with them in case the enemy dropped bombs containing poison gas.

BUS STOP

COACH STOP

FORM QUEUE
OTHER SIDE

TROOP TRANSPORT

At times, wartime roads were packed with troops travelling around the country. In the spring of 1944 the Allies prepared for D-Day – the big invasion of Europe through France.

Troops, tanks and equipment filled the roads and railways leading to the south coast. The whole of the south of England became a huge army camp. Ordinary people were not allowed to go near beaches on the east and south coasts.

Field force, 1944
A huge number of tanks is seen here lined up in a field. It took months to get all the tanks and equipment into position for the invasion of France.

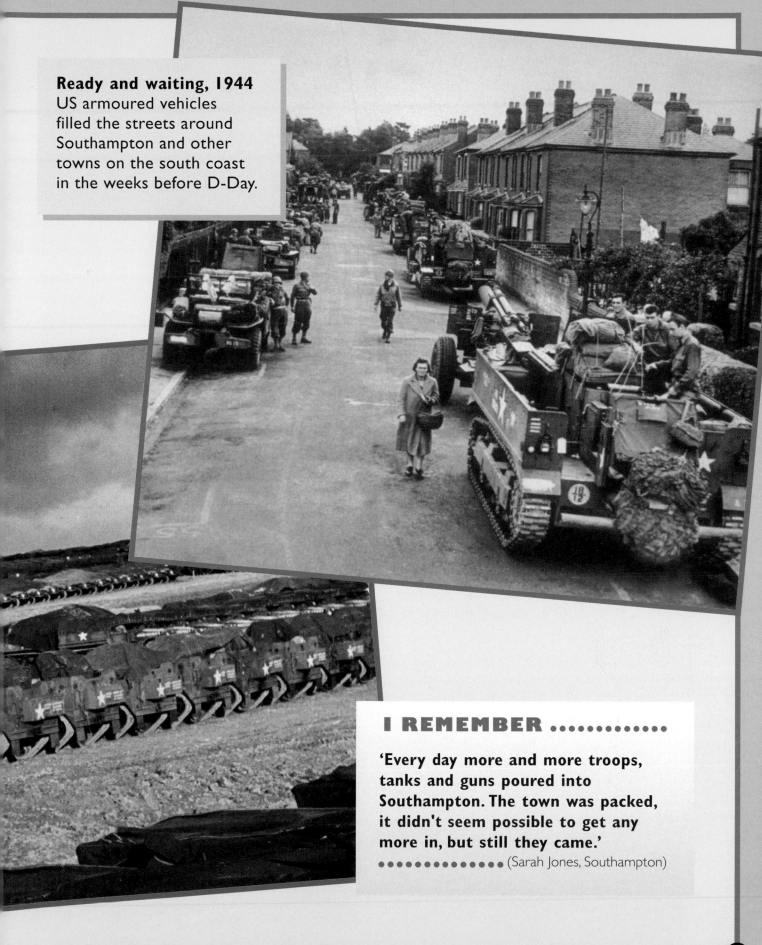

Ready and waiting, 1944
US armoured vehicles filled the streets around Southampton and other towns on the south coast in the weeks before D-Day.

I REMEMBER ....

'Every day more and more troops, tanks and guns poured into Southampton. The town was packed, it didn't seem possible to get any more in, but still they came.'
.... (Sarah Jones, Southampton)

END OF THE WAR

When the war ended in 1945, Britain had changed. Everyone wanted to build a better future.

The war brought many improvements in science and industry. Roads and railways needed to be rebuilt and modernized. Diesel trains began to take the place of steam trains. The amount of road traffic grew quickly after petrol rationing ended in 1950. New roads were built, and Britain's first motorway, the M1, was opened in 1959.

First diesel, 1948
Britain's first diesel train entered service in January 1948, just a few years after the war ended.

Motorway magic, 1959
A lot of new roads were built after the war. This is Britain's first motorway, the M1, soon after it was opened in 1959.

Back to normal, 1954
As soon as the war ended, so did the black-out. The lights of London shone out again, and traffic jams were back!

GLOSSARY

Air-raid wardens those who helped people to find shelter during air raids, gave first aid to the injured, and made sure everywhere was blacked-out

Allies the countries fighting against Germany and Japan. The main Allies were Britain and its empire, France, USA and the USSR.

Armed forces the forces to protect a country: its army, air force and navy

Black-out making sure no lights showed from houses, streets and so on, so that at night towns could not be seen from the air

Blitz the heavy bombing of Britain's towns, factories and railways by German planes in the early war years

D-Day 6 June 1944, when tens of thousands of Allied troops landed in France to begin to push the German army back into Germany

Evacuate send away for safety. Children and mothers with babies that lived in the most dangerous areas were sent to live somewhere safer.

Evacuee someone who was evacuated

Gas mask a mask that allows you to breathe without being poisoned if there is poison gas in the air

Gas practice to make sure everyone knew what to do in case of a real gas attack there were practice gas alerts

Import to buy in goods from another country to sell in your own country

Lapel labels evacuees all had a label with their name on it pinned to the front of their coat (lapel), in case they got lost

Luxury something expensive, comfortable, a treat

On leave allowed to go home from the war for a break

Rationed shared out equally among the whole population. Food, petrol and clothing were all rationed during World War Two.

Rumour something people say, or a story passing around that is not necessarily true

Traitor someone who helps the enemy and betrays his or her own country

Troops soldiers

U-Boat German submarine

FURTHER INFORMATION

Books

Butterfield, Moira, *Diary of a Young Nurse in World War II* (Franklin Watts, 2001)

Butterfield, Moira, *Going to War in World War Two* (Franklin Watts, 2002)

Cross, Vince, *Blitz: the Diary of Edie Benson, London, 1940-1941* (Scholastic 2001)

Deary, Terry, *Horrible Histories: The Woeful Second World War* (Hippo, 1999)

Hamley, Dennis, *The Second World War* (Franklin Watts, 2004)

Masters, Anthony, *World War II Stories Series* (Franklin Watts, 2004)

Reynoldson, Fiona, *The Past in Pictures: The Home Front* (Wayland, 1999)

Reynoldson, Fiona, *What Families Were Like: The Second World War* (Hodder Wayland, 2002)

Ross, Stewart, *The Blitz* (Evans, 2002)

Websites

The Home Front section of the Spartacus Second World War Encyclopedia.
http://www.spartacus.schoolnet.co.uk/2WWhome.htm

Fun interactive BBC site, in which you can pretend to go shopping in wartime Britain, read letters from evacuees and hear the sound of an air raid warning:
http://www.bbc.co.uk/history/ww2children//index.shtml

Home Sweet Home Front site containing useful information, and interesting photos and posters on various key topics: rationing, dig for victory, land girls, evacuees, squander:
http://www.homesweethomefront.co.uk/templates/hshf_frameset_tem.htm

The Second World War Experience Centre site, with descriptions of aspects of life on the home front, and memories from those who experienced it:
http://www.war-experience.org/history/keyaspects/home-british/

Wartime Memories Project. An interactive site containing questions to and answers from people who lived through World War Two:
http://www.wartimememories.co.uk/questions.html

Note to parents and teachers

Every effort has been made by the Publishers to ensure that these websites are suitable for children, that they are of the highest educational value, and that they contain no inappropriate or offensive material. However, because of the nature of the Internet, it is impossible to guarantee that the contents of these sites will not be altered. We strongly advise that Internet access is supervised by a responsible adult.

INDEX

Thanks to the Wartime Memories Project for permission to quote from its website (p. 7), and to Macmillan Children's Books, London, UK, for permission to quote from *Children of the Blitz* by Robert Westall (pp. 11, 19, 21).